Anger Management

The Mental Makeover Programme that Will Help You Take Control of Your Emotions and Achieve Freedom from Anger in Just 21 Days

(The Most Useful Guide Possible on How to Regulate Your Anxiety and Stress)

Abdullah Weigl

TABLE OF CONTENT

Has An Impact On Your Working Life And Your Professional Life. 1

Who Or What Is To Blame For The Fact That We Are So Angry? 9

Acquiring A Fundamental Knowledge Of Anger Comprehending The Components That Comprise This Emotion 18

The Perils Of Getting Angry 22

Bring Yourself Back To Your Objectives 27

What Steps Can You Take To Better Manage Your Anger? 35

The Methods That Are Used To Manage Anger 38

How Can You Control Your Angry Mood? 52

Having An Effective Handle On One's Anxiety 61

How To Eradicate Your Angry Moods By Maintaining Complete Command Over Your Emotions At All Times 65

Understanding How To Advocate For Ourselves 79

Taking Care Of Our Families And Children While Keeping Our Tempers In Check 87

Problems In Controlling One's Anger May Manifest Itself In A Variety Of Psychological Ways 95

Reformat Your Thought Process 99

Learn To Master Your Angry Feelings Before They Master You. 105

Respect For The Fury Expressed By Others . 115

Taking Pleasure In Seeing Children Thrive ... 121

Anger And Its Effects On Your Mental Health 129

The Ten-Step Process That Will Take You From Discord To Harmony 132

Tips That Will Help Your Young Child Feel Less Angry 138

You Have A Choice In How You Express Your Anger 148

Handling Children's Angry Emotions 154

The Warning Signs Of Rage That Cannot Be Suppressed 159

Your Health And Your Anger 163

Has An Impact On Your Working Life And Your Professional Life.

It would be tough for you to concentrate on your task if you are always feeling irritated. Your performance at work will suffer as a result of your persistent anger, which will in turn diminish your productivity and prevent you from achieving your objectives on time.

Constant outbursts of rage make it more difficult for you to maintain current work connections and to develop new ones. This, along with the fact that it is more difficult for you to enjoy new and improved job prospects, prevents you from making progress in your professional life.

impedes your progress in achieving your own objectives

Your capacity to concentrate on the things that are really important in life is negatively impacted when you suffer from chronic anger since all it makes you think about is the source of the issue you are experiencing. When you have trouble concentrating, you are unable to make progress toward reaching your own objectives, which prevents you from experiencing a sense of fulfillment and accomplishment in your life.

Affects one's level of contentment and emotional stability

When you are seething with rage, it is challenging to have joy and to maintain your sanity. If all you can think about is how this or that, or someone, made you angry, then you won't be able to see even the most significant benefits in your life. You will cultivate a grumbling attitude that will convert you into a whiner, someone who focuses on what is lacking or absent rather than what there is for which to be thankful. You are unable to lead a happy and meaningful life for the aforementioned reasons, in addition to this particular barrier.

You need to work on regulating your anger in healthy ways if you want to be happier, calmer, more focused, more confident, healthier, successful, and wealthy in life and if you also want to maintain healthy, pleasant relationships with other people.

The correct method to begin working toward accomplishing this objective is to first get a knowledge of the many forms of anger, choose which type best describes you, then search for the symptoms of that type. Once you have done this, you will be able to proceed to determining the causes of your anger and successfully addressing them.

The next chapter will explain how you may get started straight away with that endeavor.

There is not always anything wrong with being angry.

It is entirely normal to feel furious when unpleasant things happen to you that you didn't create and that are out of your control, as shown by the instances that have been given up to this point; thus, there is no need to feel embarrassed for experiencing anger in the present time. In addition, anger can be a constructive and beneficial feeling when it encourages individuals to speak out against injustice or to double down on their core beliefs in order to build something that is superior. There has never been a successful revolution that did not begin with fury, and there has never been a successful invention that did not begin with someone being upset with the current quo.

There is a strong probability that your anger is a sign of personal development, or at the very least that it may point out where personal growth is potential, if you discover that you are upset at something that you previously ignored without giving it a second thought. In fact, if this is the case, then your anger is a sign of personal growth. If you discover that you are becoming more and more furious at your present position without knowing why, this might be a sign that it is time to take a closer look at the way your life is currently going to ensure that you are doing all in your power to wring as much enjoyment as possible out of each day.

Because of this, it is up to each and every individual to make the decision to express their anger in ways that are constructive rather than giving in to the desire to do something that is more destructive in its place. Anger is really what you make of it, which means that it is up to each and every person to make the option to express their anger in productive ways. When you sense an outburst of rage building on, try to look at it as a source of inspiration rather than as permission to give in to your natural impulses.

The unfortunate reality is that the method of venting anger that many individuals choose to utilize often results in a myriad of problems not just in their own lives but also in the lives of others around them. Worse still, the method in which they choose to express their anger actually ends up producing more fury in a vicious self-perpetuating cycle, as the people who are the object of their wrath come to feel furious themselves as a result of the way in which they choose to display it.

The uncontrolled expression of anger is like to cancer in that it steadily spreads to affect all facets of a person's life if it is allowed to go unchecked. It may drive them to lash out at their loved ones either verbally or physically, perhaps leaving physical or emotional wounds that may never completely heal. This can cause them to lash out at their loved ones either verbally or physically. It's possible that a cocky young upstart will be able to get away with becoming furious at work at first, but you can guarantee that their career will come to a grinding halt once it becomes clear that they can't control their anger. Again, anger is not solely to blame for any of these circumstances, but it is undeniably the entry point to them. Because of this, it is imperative that you keep a close eye on your feelings of rage in order to guarantee that your responses are always constructive and helpful to all parties concerned.

Who Or What Is To Blame For The Fact That We Are So Angry?

We have previously discussed the reasons why we become angry as well as the factors that cause us to feel anger in the first place. The fundamental sensation that one has been mistreated in some way is shared by all of the many reasons why people may feel this way. And since it is irrational, anger is difficult to manage and often leads to aggressive behavior. Anger is one of the few emotions that can present itself with such force, despite the fact that no other feeling can be reasonable.

However, triggers are not the only things that might set us off; other things can also do this. In point of fact, the issue that provokes our ire may not even be all that significant; rather, it can just be the last straw that causes the camel's back to buckle. When a person is in the proper state of mind—or should I say the wrong state of mind—they have the potential to snap and abruptly fly into a blind anger. Because of this, our mental state at the time we feel ourselves becoming enraged is a vital factor to take into consideration.

We are sensitive to feelings and emotions.

Let's imagine something occurred in your personal life; I'm absolutely certain that you are extremely acquainted with the way that you feel when anything like this occurs. Possibly you are going through a breakup, or perhaps you are having a disagreement with someone who is important to you. Perhaps a member of your family is sick or is going through a particularly difficult time. Perhaps it's because of anything that took place at work. The fact that it has a significant effect on your emotions is what really matters here, not the reason why it has that effect.

And while you are fretting over the circumstance, silently suffering, driving yourself insane with ideas and potential outcomes, and working on finding a solution, someone sets you off. It may have been something utterly harmless, like slamming a door too harshly or grabbing something from your desk without asking first. There's also the possibility that it's something more significant, but even so, it wouldn't generally be enough to make you lose your cool.

But now, now you have to take into consideration your sensitive and emotional condition; you're weak and worn out, and the simplest thing might be the one that pushes you over the edge, the one that is too much for you to manage. You will lose your cool when that unfortunate event ultimately takes place. You may not always be angry at the person who deserves it, but you've been bottling up all of these feelings inside of you, and now they've finally exploded.

How the Feeling of Anger Can Rule Your Life

Your life might become fully consumed by your anger. It has the potential to change who you are and separate you from the people who are closest to you, including friends and family. The point is, at first, you will not be able to perceive the grasps of rage that are being exerted. Your thoughts might convince you that becoming upset is the appropriate response to a certain circumstance. Because of the things that have happened to you in the past and the experiences that you have had, you could get the impression that anger is the solution to your issues rather than the underlying cause of them. Before you realize it, the feeling takes over your life and becomes the only thing you are familiar with. It utterly paralyzes you.

The inability to control one's anger may be the downfall of a relationship as well as a career. It is also possible for it to result in more severe events, such as the victim being hurt by another person or the offender being arrested for harming another individual. It is possible for someone to cause more than one death at once when they let anger, which is a potentially deadly emotion, drive their actions. There have been cases in which people have been killed because of their anger.

There are situations in which rage might result in one's becoming embarrassed in front of others. Some individuals are prone to having emotional breakdowns and embarrassing themselves by shouting, crying, and behaving like children when they do so. There is a possibility that you may get into a brawl at a local establishment that, after the fight, you will not want to visit again. If you get into a heated argument with a colleague, it might potentially damage your reputation at work as well.

There is also a section on Reddit dedicated to "public freak-outs," which displays recordings of individuals having meltdowns in public owing to an eruption of wrath. A good number of these videos were captured in public places, such as a quick-service restaurant or a well-known retail establishment. The majority of the time, it concerns those who have the perception that they have been treated unjustly in some way. They may not have been eligible for a discount, for example, or their meal could have been served at an unacceptable pace. In any case, they are rather little occurrences that have no business inciting someone to intense rage.

The videos of these irate individuals are then uploaded on the internet so that everyone may make fun of them. It is correct to say that these expressions of passion are ridiculous and should not be done in public. On the other hand, they always have more fundamental problems that dictate how they respond to a given situation. People who fit this description most typically experience aspects of life that defy their ability to make sense of them and struggle with issues they cannot influence.

The irritation and the misunderstanding sparked the fury. When they are confronted with a circumstance that can be readily identified as being one that creates legitimate anger, then that style of expression will become their go-to choice. Consider the situation of a guy who has just been fired from his job, separated from his wife, and is coping with a bad situation all at the same time, for instance. The next day, he went to have a coffee as usual, but when he placed his drink order, the waitress brought him the incorrect beverage. The fact that the guy has to wait once again in order to get the appropriate beverage is likely to aggravate him more.

It is appropriate to see this situation as a rather minor nuisance at this point. After all, waiting is something that nobody enjoys doing. However, instead of venting his frustration in a subdued manner, he lashes out at the employees at the coffee shop, tosses the drink at them, and then rushes out of the establishment while muttering awful things. He is not unhappy with them because they messed up his order; rather, he is angry with his manager, his wife, and the world in general. The guy is unable to fathom some of the sentiments that going through a divorce or losing one's job might bring, but he is aware of how frustrating it can be to be served the incorrect beverage.

Therefore, the man's thinking convinces him that lashing out in anger is the acceptable way to respond to the situation. Because the circumstance is not difficult to handle, he has a sense of mastery over it. It may also offer him a surge of adrenaline, and as a result, it provides him with the brief reprieve that he so badly needs from the larger problems that are plaguing his life.

The way other people see you might shift when you're angry. It is possible that they will refrain from telling you some things because they do not want to see an angry reaction from you. Everyone, at some point or another, is in possession of a secret, but they are too embarrassed to share it with you. Because of this, everyone works together secretly behind your back to address the problem before you ever realize what's going on. When you become aware of a scenario like this, it may be painful as well as humiliating for you.

Acquiring A Fundamental Knowledge Of Anger Comprehending The Components That Comprise This Emotion

How can we define anger?

Anger is an emotion that may seem quite different on different people depending on the circumstances. It might be anything from a little annoyance to a full-blown wrath. People, similar to other feelings, also experience equivalent changes in their bodies, as shown by the following signs:

a rapid and irregular heartbeat, as well as elevated blood pressure

Alterations in one's hormonal levels; more specifically, an increase in the levels of adrenaline and cortisol in the affected individual

A discernible shift in both the speaker's tone of voice and look on their face

What are some reasons why a person could get angry?

Because feelings are experienced differently by different people, there is no one exact circumstance that may cause an angry reaction in any individual. After all, the feeling might be affected by both internal and exterior influences at the same time. Nonetheless, there are two kinds of circumstances in general that have a high probability of making a person angry:

If the individual feels that the scenario poses a risk to their safety or image (as when a person driving recklessly nearly struck them), they may choose to avoid the situation.

if the circumstance has the potential to prevent the person from carrying out their plan or living up to their expectations (for example, running into heavy traffic shortly before an important meeting at which you cannot afford to be late).

How can one show their anger?

Anger is what provides a person the energy to be able to deal with a difficult circumstance and fend off a danger to their safety or security when they feel that their safety or security is in jeopardy. As a result, an individual's response becomes more violent when they are angry. In this setting, the ability to control your wrath is essential to your life.

On the other hand, this feeling has the potential to become negative if the person experiencing it is unable to exercise self-control and allows themselves to be overcome by the intensity of their emotions. After all, you can't always utilize that energy to get even with someone else until the feeling passes, can you? Therefore, it is important for the individual to acquire the skills necessary to vent their frustration in a way that is neither hostile nor damaging.

The Perils Of Getting Angry

An old proverb states that "anger is an acid that can do more harm to the vessel in which it is stored than to anything on which it is poured." Fury has the potential to ruin a great number of fulfilling futures.

1. Your own sense of well-being will suffer if you give in to anger.

The emotions of pleasure and tranquility are both undermined and ultimately destroyed by the negative effects of anger. People who are in a fury are unable to think rationally for this reason. When they are upset, no one can experience inner serenity.

2. Being angry may be stressful since, according to medical professionals, when we are angry, our blood pressure often rises up. Bitterness, according to

Maya Angelou, is analogous to cancer. It does its digestion on the host. However, rage is like a raging fire. It destroys everything in a clean fire." The negative effects of stress on health might be exacerbated by anger.

3. Being angry might cause one to become bitter and unable to forgive.

A pastor friend of mine who had a heart ailment once told me that all of the efforts by medical specialists to help him regain his health failed miserably until he forgave his father, whom he had been furious with. His health started to worsen before he made the decision to forgive his father in his heart.

Many individuals are preoccupied with drug usage, but this has no impact on their illness. This is because the origin of their illness is rooted in their anger, which has resulted in bitterness and an inability to forgive. Because of this, there is a proverb that states, "Anger is often more hurtful than the injury that caused it."

4. Feeling angry is like having a friend in the long arm of the law.

When resentment is fostered in any situation, the authorities are put on high alert to deal with the situation. Because of the activities they committed while angry, a great number of individuals have been arrested, prosecuted, and given heavy sentences. Because of their rage, some people have been waiting for their trials for years now.

My buddy is a pastor and he went to 'Kirikiri' to do prison evangelism there. He related to me a tale about a conversation he had with an inmate on one of his visits to the facility. He was delivering the word of God to the convicts who were waiting trial, and he saw that one of the detainees was sobbing uncontrollably as he was doing so. My acquaintance added that he knew deep down that he was not sobbing out of conviction for the message that he was delivering, which is why he was crying.

So when he completed his message, he went up to him and wanted to know why he was sobbing while he was ministering. This happened just after he concluded his speech. The guy of middle age reassured him that he was not an awful human being. He claimed to be a bricklayer working for one of his clients who had engaged him to do something for him. He stated the customer had hired him to do something for him. Then, suddenly, a young guy appeared out of nowhere and started dragging his shovel behind him. He said that the other individual asserted that the shovel was his property. A brawl broke out in the middle of the heated dispute that was going on. He used the stick to strike the young guy, causing him to pass away instantaneously. Because of this, he was sentenced to time behind bars. He said that he has been detained at that location for a considerable amount of time, but that his case has not yet been heard.

It has been said that "if you are patient in one moment of anger, you will escape a hundred days of sorrow." This is a true statement. We pray that the LORD bestows upon us the knowledge and grace to figure out how to react to those who want to provoke and anger us.

Bring Yourself Back To Your Objectives

Your objectives are to exercise self-control over your anger, refrain from acting irrationally, and let go of any unpleasant ideas that come to mind. To put this into practice, whenever you find yourself in a difficult situation or if anything causes you to lose control of your temper, stop for a second and allow yourself some time to reflect before you react. Make an effort to look on the bright side of the situation at hand. Are you irritated by the behavior of a certain individual in your life? Why not give them the benefit of the doubt and assume the best about them? It's possible that you're misinterpreting the signals. Always allow some time for reflection before reacting to a situation in order to prevent creating unneeded confusion.

Nobody is without flaws. You will never be perfect, and there is no guarantee that you will always be able to keep your temper in check. That's not a problem. Within each of us is a war that has to be fought. Therefore, when you make a mistake and are unable to keep your anger under control, pause for a while and think about it. Try not to give up. It is not a simple task, and it is reasonable to expect difficulty. Think on the positive things you've done and the accomplishments you've attained, no matter how big or how minor they may seem. Do you remember how you were able to maintain your composure despite the fact that you were insulted? How about the patience you shown while waiting in the huge queue at the coffee shop? Think about how far you've come in terms of achievement, but also about all that has in store for you in the future.

In addition, it is essential to review your objectives and make certain that they are not just SMART but that you are also well on your way to accomplishing them. SMART is an acronym that stands for "Specific, Measurable, Achievable, Relevant, and Time-Bound." This approach proposes that all objectives should be attainable, specific, quantifiable, relevant, and have a strict timeframe that cannot be easily adjusted. This makes certain that the objectives you choose to pursue are going to be genuinely deserving of both your time and the work that you intend to put in to making them a reality.

Your first SMART goal should be one that is simple enough to assure that you will accomplish it, while also being pertinent enough to your day-to-day life that achieving it will serve as an easy reminder to you that you are capable of achieving objectives. This kind of goal is known as a "starter" goal. This manner, you will begin establishing the appropriate brain pathways as soon as possible, which will then form into patterns, which will ultimately become habits. This will allow you to create the neural pathways as quickly as possible. Keeping this in mind, you should begin by setting a goal that is at least somewhat associated with the destructive tendency that you are the most eager to alter in your life. At this stage, you don't need to have a specific objective in mind; all you need is the kernel of an idea that you may develop into something more substantial in the future. Take into consideration the following in order to confirm that you are moving in the proper direction.

When a goal is defined, it may have quantifiable points of accomplishment, and as a result, it is far more likely to be realized than when the objective is vague. When deciding on particular objectives, you should constantly ask yourself the following question: Who can assist you in achieving the goal? What is the particular aim that you have for the goal? Where is it that you can accomplish the objective? When do you anticipate that the task will be finished? Which limitations, if any, stand between you and achieving the goal? Why do you feel it is important for you to achieve the goal? Answers to all six questions should be included in good objectives.

Measurable: A good objective should have clear metrics that succinctly indicate success or failure so that you can readily confirm that you are on the correct track. Metrics may be broken down into percentages, dollars, or other units of measurement. By keeping track of how far along you are in the process, you may ensure that important milestones, such as achieving particular deadlines or meeting due dates, are not missed. This feeling of continual advancement is essential to any endeavor that is pursued over the long term. Make use of percentages and elements that can be measured, such as raising your daily reading time to thirty minutes or your revenue by ten percent.

Attainable: A good goal is one that you can have reasonable possibility of achieving if you put in the necessary amount of work. This indicates that you would want to choose a target that is neither too simple nor too challenging for you to achieve. Setting objectives that are too easy won't get you the kind of outcomes you want, and setting goals that are too difficult to achieve will guarantee that you will ultimately lose motivation. The most fruitful course of action will always be one that falls somewhere in the center.

Realistic: It is crucial to bear in mind any present barriers on your path to success when creating objectives. These roadblocks may prohibit you from fulfilling goals in the manner in which they were intended. On paper, you could have the ability to achieve a goal, but the reality of the situation you find yourself in can make it impossible for you to do so right now. If you want the finest possible outcomes, you should choose objectives that can really be achieved in light of the present circumstances.

Aptly timed: A goal that is open-ended is one that will never be accomplished in its entirety. When planning out your objectives, it is essential that you leave yourself just enough time to achieve them if you are willing to put in a little more effort. When things start to become difficult, having this additional drive will make it much simpler to stay going. Make sure you use the correct times or dates.

What Steps Can You Take To Better Manage Your Anger?

You have found the proper spot to find out how to assist if you believe that you or someone around you may have some difficulties with anger, and if you believe that someone else may have problems in this sector as well.

When you find yourself in a position where you feel like lashing out in wrath, you may go to this chapter for some tried-and-true strategies and activities that can assist you in maintaining control of your emotions.

Rule No. 1: Determine the rationale for your irrational outbursts.

You are on your way to the workplace when all of a sudden, you are stuck in the midst of a massive traffic snarl that is completely out of character for your trip. You are beginning to feel frustrated and furious as a natural response to the circumstances. Your degree of wrath rises to the point that you can sense the beginning stages of a full-blown rage.

Take a minute to step away from what you're doing right now and ask yourself, "Why am I getting so angry?" Is your annoyance really brought on by the backup in traffic, or is there another factor at play here? It's possible that you got off to a rough start today since you couldn't get much sleep the night before. It's possible that you skipped breakfast since you were in such a rush to get ready in the morning. It's possible that you have an overwhelming number of urgent tasks requiring your immediate attention waiting for you in the workplace. The majority of the time, the cause that is making you furious is not the one that is immediately apparent; rather, it is a reason that is concealed and requires some reflection to uncover.

Do you know someone who has a short fuse all the time? Is he or she always irritable, yelling and verbally assaulting others to the point that they inspire terror in other people? Investigate any possible explanations beyond the ones that the individual is displaying openly. People are often not irate over the traffic bottleneck, the burned toast, or the missing handbag; rather, it is likely something more personal that is the source of their ire. Did the individual spend their youth in a home where they were subjected to abuse? Is their romantic partnership going through a rough patch right now? Is it true that they are suffering money problems? Is there anything that continues to annoy them? If you can discover their true motivation, you will be able to teach them (or yourself) how to better manage their anger.

The Methods That Are Used To Manage Anger

It has at long last come to pass. People have been trying your patience, and you believe that you have every right to be upset with them since you have every reason to be. So, here's the deal: resist the urge to give in and take action instead. You may avoid complete anarchy by following these preventative measures, which are outlined below.

Bring people's attention to your feelings of rage. This is the very first action that has to be taken. Because anger is an emotion that is fueled by impulsive behavior, the most effective strategy for overcoming it is to acknowledge its presence. In point of fact, many forms of hostility, particularly in public settings, have a tendency to stop when other people draw attention to it. In this instance, you need to bring your own anger to your notice in order to halt what would otherwise be an unregulated response to the circumstance.

Tuning into the influence your anger has on your body may help you accomplish this goal. It manifests itself somewhat differently in various persons, although in most cases it manifests as a tightness of the muscles or other regions of the body. Check your face and your hands to determine whether they are becoming more tense; your face should also feel more constricted. Concentrating only on these things will divert your attention away from the impulsive violence.

Take some time to consider the source of your anger. There is a very good possibility that whatever it is to which you are responding is not anything that should warrant you losing your cool about it. Put the following questions to yourself:

What level of significance does this whole matter have for me? Should I be indignant about it? Is it anything that warrants my losing my patience?

Do I have this circumstance properly figured out, or am I missing anything important? Did the persons who were engaged want to get under my skin?

Is reacting angrily the proper course of action? What do you expect the results to be? What is it that I really want to achieve by responding in this manner?

I guess it's time for me to vent a little bit of my rage. Should I direct my ire on this person or this situation?

These questions are designed to provoke you to pause and give some thought to the answers, despite the fact that they are logical. At this point, your anger should have already begun to abate to a considerable degree.

Enjoy some time off. No, this does not imply that you take a vacation at this time. When things start to become heated up, people will understand if you go away for a little while and let things calm down a little bit before you return. This provides you with the opportunity to think about what you ought to do about the circumstance in peace (i.e., without having to put up with the pressure of the people around you). It is possible that spending some time by yourself will be sufficient to provide you with a new viewpoint that will assist you in finding a solution to the issue. You wouldn't believe how much can be accomplished in only five minutes for you.

Rest and relax. You may want to give any of these strategies a try when you're taking a break since they have the potential to help relieve some of the tension:

Take a few deep breaths. Take a deep breath in and let the oxygen to circulate through your body; this will help to reduce the tension that is around your muscles and will enable you to think more clearly.

Stretch out your muscles and get some exercise. Put your anger toward something that will truly help you feel better without putting you in danger. Pull out a stress ball and give it a good squeezing, or you could just do some easy stretches wherever you are. It doesn't have to be anything complex; it simply has to be enough to help you take out some of that pent-up tension.

You should recite specific mantras to yourself repeatedly. More than merely giving you a feeling of encouragement, telling yourself to "calm down" or that "you can do this" has a multiplicative effect. Choose and use whichever approach is successful for you.

Try to balance on only one foot. This may seem ridiculous, but in reality, it makes it very difficult to become furious in this manner.

Take in some musical sounds. Everyone has a rhythm that helps them relax when they're feeling anxious.

There is such a wide variety of outlets available for venting all of that frustration. You only have to choose the strategy that is most effective for you and make a mental note to put it into action whenever the situation calls for it.

Give yourself space and time to reflect on what caused the reaction.

It's possible that buying some time is the only way to stop a furious response in its tracks. It's possible that the solution is as simple as taking a few steps.

When confronted with a trigger, it's possible that it will be helpful to:

- Count from one to 10.

- Go for a brisk little walk.

- Get in touch with someone who hasn't responded straight away, such a close friend, a member of your family, or a professional counselor.

There is a possibility that it will be useful to orally explain the concepts that are motivating the anger to someone who is not the subject of the feeling.

This could help defuse the situation and zero in on the cause of the intense feelings that people are experiencing.

Make use of strategies that can assist you in better managing your anger.

These things could help a person relax or distract their attention for a short period of time, giving them the opportunity to process their thoughts in a constructive way.

Finding a method that works for you might be beneficial in calming down when you're furious, but everyone responds favorably to a different set of techniques in this regard.

Among the several methods that are employed are:

• Breathe in deeply and slowly, concentrating on each breath as it comes in and goes out, and making an effort to exhale more than you take in.

• To alleviate the effects of stress on your body, try tensing and then relaxing every part of your body for the duration of the count of ten.

- Mindfulness: One technique that falls under the category of mindfulness is meditation. With enough practice, this technique may assist in diverting attention away from feelings of anger when a trigger event occurs.

- Exercise: Exercising is one of the best ways to get rid of any excess adrenaline in your system. Aggressive or confrontational feelings may be effectively released via the practice of combat sports such as boxing or martial arts, as well as through vigorous running or walking.

- Look for other methods to release your anger. Tearing up newspaper, smashing ice cubes over a sink, or beating or yelling into a pillow are all examples of methods of releasing anger that do not cause harm to other people.

- Concoct distractions: Techniques like as dancing to uplifting music, taking a calming shower, or producing, fixing, writing, or drawing might help you move away from the situation by providing you with a distraction.

When expressing disapproval with a group member, it might be helpful to plan out what to say ahead of time. This could make it easier to keep the discussion on topic and on track, and it might also make it less likely that anger will be directed in the wrong direction.

Focusing on potential solutions to problems, rather than the problems themselves, increases the likelihood that a satisfactory resolution will be reached and reduces the likelihood that an angry reaction will be given.

Additionally important to one's mental and physical health is maintaining a sleep routine that allows for at least seven hours of restful sleep every night. According to a number of studies, not getting enough sleep may lead to a number of different health problems, including irritation and aggression.

How Can You Control Your Angry Mood?

If you want to assist with spotting the indications and signs of stun and handling triggers in a great approach, you may use the Shock the Board, which consists of a number of capabilities. It is necessary for a private individual to suppress their curiosity throughout the design stage of the technique strategy and to communicate their requirements while remaining quiet and knowledgeable.

The act of directing amazement precludes either holding it in or remaining far from sentiments associated to it.

It's possible that adjusting to amazement is a skill that can be learnt, and that practically everyone can learn the best way to maintain control of their emotions given enough time, effort, and responsibility. At the point in time whilst resentment is adversely affecting a courting, and in particular in the occasion that it's far inciting horrible or regardless risky lead, a person may additionally moreover advantage by means of advising a mental health hold close or getting to a resentment the heads category. In spite of this, there are straightforward and speedy methods by which a person, a group of people, or even three people may learn that they can resolve such difficulties without the need for professional assistance.

Keeping one's cool while one is furious

Psyche, which is a significant intellectual properly being respectable element in the uk, believes that there are three guideline reviews for regulating stun:

• Be aware of the warning signals of paralysis. • Ground oneself in the actual world in order to gain control over the triggers.

• Follow the steps that will assist you in maintaining your composure under the ridicule.

Vision astounds

When this point has passed, it is often difficult to end the stun instantly. Having said that, recognizing the feeling when it first arises is often really important. This is so despite the fact that it would also moreover occur. It is possible for a person to redirect their course of instinct to a location that is more helpful because of it. The body goes through a series of physical reactions when it is stunned. It causes the body to produce adrenaline, which is known as the "fight or flight" hormone because it prepares a person for potentially dangerous situations.

This may have the following effects: a rapid pulse; a quicker loosening up; tension throughout the body; impatience; pacing; and tapping the feet; holding the fingers hands and jaw; sweating; and trembling.

The occurrence of these bodily repercussions may herald the beginning of an appropriate response to a situation of events. In any event, being aware of the symptoms and indications at an early stage might provide a person with the opportunity to evaluate whether or not the cause justifies this bodily response.

In the event that this is the case, they could then be in a position to find a way to influence their bodily weight.

Getting a degree after dropping out

Getting some time to yourself is something that should be done every once in a while in order to prevent an angry response. This is something that may be included in the number one measures. It is helpful to: Right even though extended far past seeking with a rationale, it is helpful to:

- start at one and count to ten

- pass for a brisk walk around the park

- Acquaint yourself with a person who isn't immediately covered, such as a partner, a member of the family, or a teacher.

When speaking to a member of the public who is not a participant in the convergence of the answer, it might be helpful to verbally skim over the considerations that led to the failure. This may assist diffuse the situation and ensure that everyone has a clearer understanding of the thought process that should be used for the special assessments. Keep up social activities, such as the Crisis text line, are available to provide assistance to residents of the United States who are having difficulty expressing their displeasure.

They assist us in determining appropriate actions.

When it comes to making any kind of choice, the weight of your feelings can't be understated. The manner you choose to respond to whatever feelings you're experiencing is a direct reflection of those feelings. It is possible for a person to lose their capacity to feel emotions if they suffer from a certain kind of brain injury. Research has shown that persons with this handicap have a difficult time making judgments that are logically sound. This is a problem for them.

Empathy is born out of feelings.

Emotions also help you understand other people, and the way you communicate your feelings to other people is a key factor in determining how well they comprehend your state of mind. In a similar vein, paying great attention to a person's expressions of emotion might provide you with more insight on how they are feeling. Having such an in-depth awareness of the feelings of other people enables you to form great connections with those individuals.

Controlling One's Emotions

There are a variety of cues that might let us in on how another person is experiencing their emotions. Body language and the manner in which they express themselves are the two aspects that are most significant. It might be in the manner that they are speaking, or it could be in the emotions that they have on their faces. Because communication isn't always verbal, it's important to pay attention to a person's facial expressions and the way they move their body. More than eighty percent of communication is done without words being spoken.

It is vital that we comprehend that we are able to exert control over our feelings. It isn't always essential for our emotions to govern us. We have some control over it. Emotions are a double-edged sword: on the one hand, they are beneficial to us in a variety of ways, but on the other, they may be detrimental to our mental health if we do not deal with them effectively. Because of the strong connection that exists between our mental and physical health, our feelings have the ability to influence our whole existence. You should never pass judgment on your feelings since they are not the same thing as your identity. They are only feelings, and they come and go at random. You have the ability to exercise regulation and command over them. Everyone is free to choose how they would want to proceed in this situation. You only need to develop a heightened awareness of them.

Having An Effective Handle On One's Anxiety

As a human being, one of the normal feelings that you are able to experience is worry or anxiety. Despite this, you should not give in to it or let it control you in any way. Even if the vast majority of the things that are causing you anxiety will not come to pass, you spend a significant amount of time worrying and being worried about them. The following is a list of things that you can do to help control your anxiety.

Put your worries into categories.

Make a note of the items and occurrences in your life that give you anxiety, using a pen and paper. Put them in one of two categories: "can change" and "cannot change." Write down your worries in the "can change" column, such as the possibility of losing your job due to frequent tardiness and absenteeism, your fear of public speaking, and your concerns about your financial situation. Write down your worries about things that are beyond your control in the "cannot change" column, such as poor weather, the end of the planet, or your own mortality.

Find answers to the concerns that are really bothering you.

Because of your categorization, you should now be aware of which concerns you no longer need to be concerned about. These are the worries that you can't do anything about at this point. Instead, you should focus on finding answers to your actual worries. You will need to get up earlier in the morning if you want to rid yourself of the anxiety caused by your concern that you will be fired due of your chronic tardiness and absence from work. Speaking in front of an audience is something that was covered in the chapter before this one. The answer is to fully prepare for it and see it as a challenge that you should gladly embrace. This is the solution.

Put an end to unnecessary anxiety about the things you are unable to alter, and put an end to 'false' fears about those things. Your life will become more stressful if you continue to worry about them. You would waste your time worrying about things over which you have no control, rather than experiencing life to its fullest extent. What a pointless use of time. Because life is so brief, you need to make the most of it by getting out there and having fun.

You are unable to determine the exact moment that you will pass away, therefore you should quit thinking about it. You will not be able to stop

Armageddon from happening, even if it does, so try not to worry yourself to death by replaying in your head all the horrific scenarios you've seen in movies.

In this particular setting, your only choice is to accept the situation as it is. You have no choice but to come to terms with the truth that you are powerless against them and give in to the inevitable sequence of events. When you do, it will be much simpler for you to quit being concerned about them.

How To Eradicate Your Angry Moods By Maintaining Complete Command Over Your Emotions At All Times

When it comes to rage, the single most crucial thing to keep in mind is that you should never act when you're furious. You'll have the sudden need to take action and demonstrate that you've learned your lesson. However, this is just your wrath taking control of you.

When you become furious, your body releases a hormone known as the emergency hormone, which is also known as the flight or fight hormone. This is the root cause of your intense desire to get revenge on your kid, by the way. But please just wait a moment. You may still demonstrate your mastery of the material in the future, although in a calmer and more controlled manner.

Take into consideration the following:

Specifically, what is it that you hope will be passed on to your children from you?

Would you want kids to learn that shouting, screaming, insulting one another, slapping one another, or striking out in humiliating ways is a healthy way to express one's anger?

Or, would you rather serve as an example to them that, despite the fact that experiencing rage is a natural part of the human condition, being level-headed and in charge of one's emotions in the face of anger is the goal that every responsible person should strive for?

If you want to maintain your composure and respond to challenging circumstances in a manner that is noticeably more productive and reflective of your maturity level, then the following are some strategies that may help you...

9 Powerful Methods That Will Help You Always Keep Your Emotional Composure

1.) Tell People What You Want Instead of Getting Angry:

When we lose our temper with our children, it is often always because we failed to establish appropriate limits for them.

For example, let's assume you've just had a hard and stressful day, and now that you're home to get some much-needed rest, but their carefree loudness is keeping you from having a peaceful experience. It would be more effective to call them together, let them know you had a busy day, and urge them to keep their play in control so as not to disturb your serenity. Instead of becoming furious and shouting at them to stop, it would be more effective to become angry yourself and yell at them to stop.

When you let rid of your anger and go at your children, they are more likely to react positively to an open and honest heart-to-heart conversation in which you reiterate your expectations of them in a calm and loving manner.

2.) Before you do anything else, be sure you have regained your composure:

If you are feeling upset, you need to find a technique to calm yourself down before you do anything else. Always keep in mind that the harmful words you speak to your children or the punishment you mete out on them because of your wrath are things that can never be taken back.

Having a strong sense of self-awareness will always help you gain a better handle on your feelings. Ask yourself: "Do you really want to allow your feelings to take control of your life?" If the answer is no, then you need to find a technique to relax your anxieties. You may do this by taking a few slow, deep breaths, moving away from the situation, becoming involved in other activities only to divert yourself, counting to one hundred in your head before acting, biting your tongue and holding it in for a few minutes until you are calm before uttering a word, or counting to one hundred in your mind before acting. Even if you have to force yourself to grin, this will convey a signal to your nervous system that there is no immediate threat, and this will start to calm you down.

Understand that every time you successfully restrain yourself from acting out of anger, you are training your brain to have better self control when faced with similar challenges in the future.

3. Give Yourself a Break: Whenever you find yourself becoming frustrated or angry in the middle of a challenging circumstance, it is important to step away for a few minutes and collect your thoughts. Instead of responding to the trigger, give yourself some space and time away from the incident, and then come back to it when you are in a state that is more calm and in control of your emotions.

If you really have to, get some distance from your child physically so that you won't be tempted to lash out in anger.

Getting some distance from the conflict does not indicate that your kid has triumphed over the issue. It only demonstrates to them how to exercise self-control and remain in command of their surroundings.

While you are gone, try not to dwell on the current predicament too much since doing so may just serve to aggravate you more.

4.) Give Voice to Your Fury While Refraining From Acting On It:

It's possible that you won't always be able to control what your children do, but you have complete command over how you respond to anything they do.

Controlling how much anger you show is an effective strategy for dealing with it. When you are in a lot better emotional state, you will be able to go over precisely what the children did that got on your nerves, and you will be able to devise a method that is efficient for dealing with it.

After giving it a lot of thought, you may come to the conclusion that in order to stop a recurrence of the incident, you either need to be stricter with the rules before they get out of hand, get closer to your children so that they can have more faith in you and be more candid with you about their worries, requirements, and goals, or work things out with your partner so that they can pitch in and assist you with things more frequently than they currently do.

It is easier to maintain control of the situation and come up with more effective strategies to deal with it if you listen to your anger rather than just acting on it when it arises.

RESPONDING IN A DIFFERENT MANNER; WE ARE NO LONGER SIMPLY REACTING

Now that we have established the new ground control center for regulating our anger, we are free to go out into the world and express ourselves and behave anyway we choose without as much concern that we may unintentionally turn into wrath machines. By practicing attentive awareness, we were able to reset the bodily system. We have retrained the mind system in order to give it greater agency and expertise in the selection of ideas as well as the coupling of thoughts and emotions. We have devised a method of inside communication that is predicated on the practice of attentive awareness. Through this method, we will establish and reset the intention to maintain our focus on our various states of body and thoughts. Now we are aware that our body and mental states come, we are aware that they change, and we are aware that they go.

How does each of these things express itself as a distinct response?

It may be summed up using only two words, which we are already familiar with: the pause. Everything that we have studied up to this point has prepared us for this. When we don't give ourselves time to reflect before acting, we are, by definition, just responding. The pause is where all of life's most precious treasures are kept. The pause gives us the opportunity to prevent ourselves from acting in a way that is dictated by our reptilian brain and that we may later come to regret. Taking a moment to reflect allows for the development of insights that may help drive a more sensible reaction later on. The pause provides us with the opportunity to think of a brand new way to answer, as well as a brand new way to both talk and behave.

The emotion of rage is always present in our lives.

The feeling of anger is quite natural in humans. A great number of individuals have come to believe that the word "anger" can only ever refer to "rage." In point of fact, fury may be described using a variety of different terms, including wrath. Rage may be located on the higher end of our 0 to 10 scale, which represents a continuum. In addition, I'm going to venture a guess and suggest that anger in and of itself is a natural feeling experienced by humans. Every one of us has struggled with problems, experienced events, or been victimized in ways that have caused us to feel anger that is weighted more heavily toward the extreme end of the scale. It is natural, and it reflects the human condition.

The capacity for insight, the ability to make reasonable judgments and choices, and the capacity to apply mindfulness to our physical sensations, our emotions, and our thinking processes are three further characteristics that are unique to humans. As we are forced to confront the reality of our anger on a daily basis, it is imperative that we respect it and communicate to the part of ourselves that experiences it that we are aware of it and are able to deal with intense feelings. If we are able to bring attention to the aspect of our anger that is the most potent—our rage—then we will be able to work our way down and acquire mindfulness of the aspects of our anger that are less potent. In addition, if we are aware of the many expressions and intensities of anger in this manner, we will be able to handle any and all of these aspects of anger at any given moment.

If we accept the fact that we will have to deal with rage on a daily basis, we will be able to take both immediate and long-term actions to support our efforts. In the near term, we want to be able to create a pause between emotions, ideas, and actions via the use of methods that can be used immediately, such as the ones that we have established with our emergency advice and the utilization of the rage scale. In addition to this, one of our long-term goals is to continue bringing down the rate at which we are angry at rest. Since we are aware that we will experience anger on a daily basis, why not work toward reducing its impact on our lives so that we may begin each day at a lower point on the anger scale? If we do things in this manner, there will be less of a chance that we will go up the scale into more perilous terrain, where we may have less control over our activities.

We will find that we are able to live with our partners, our families, our workplaces, our trips to the grocery store, and our drives on the freeway—all of our relationships and our daily interactions—while also feeling at peace with ourselves and others if we use a combination of mindfulness skills that address our in-the-moment struggles and an ongoing program of teaching our body, mind, and spirit to lower our breathing rate, our heart rate, and our blood pressure.

Understanding How To Advocate For Ourselves

Professionals are aware that rage may mask feelings of strain.

The expression "gloom can be a concealment for anger," which is an old psychotherapy aphorism concerning unaware mental barriers, also says that anger can mask despair. In a similar fashion, we may inadvertently feel uneasy about our heated feelings, and similarly, we may unknowingly feel furious about being on the edge of our emotions.

As advisors, we make an effort to disclose this information to our clients; however, it is frequently a difficult offer because people do not have the habit of questioning the feelings that they are communicating and considering whether or not they may be a swap for other, more difficult to tolerate feelings.

When seen from the outside, it is sometimes easy to see that a guy who is angry may truly have something to be agitated about... nevertheless, this is not at all clear to the person who is in the throes of rage at the time. There is a reasonable explanation justification that lies behind this.

A single representative example

Recent events in my own life have driven this point home to me in a very clear and compelling way.

When I was in the car, it skidded out of control on the ice that was on the parkway about ten years ago, or somewhere around there. Even though no one was wounded in the incident, it left me with the strongly experienced notion that it was very risky to drive in the winter when the weather was freezing. At the point when my better half insisted a couple of weeks earlier on making such an exertion across the mountains in winter... I was aware on purpose that I thought it was premature. I also turned out to be really irate with him and, in all honesty, I was a bit of a diva, looking for someone to blame and arguing over every aspect of the prearranged journey. My pessimism and wrath continued to rise steadily until the point that I had to flee, and even after that. In spite of the fact that a change in the weather was forecast, the chilly circumstances that we encountered when we first started out did little to improve my mood. My dissatisfied spouse at one time suggested that they should just leave me and go live on the street.

Because I hadn't gotten enough sleep the night before the trip, I found myself dozing asleep at some point when we were in the car. When I woke up thirty minutes after the event, the weather had already cleared up, and the roads were in pristine condition and dry. When the unease that was causing the road conditions to deteriorate went away, I was astounded to see that my terrible anger had melted away just as completely as the snow.

It was at precisely that moment that I at last purposefully recognized that the fury I had been displaying was really a cover for my anxiety... in addition, it was at precisely that moment that I also recognized how absolutely convincing the appearance of rage had been.

Interestingly, a week later when I was supposed to set off spontaneously for a trip in circumstances that were somewhat comparable, I felt quite confident (as I was in full control of the option to go or not), and it was my spouse's concern for my wellness on the journey that was interpreted as anger by me. In a humorous way, it seemed as if he was annoyed that I was not pessimistic or anxious about going out alone since I had gone on in such a serious manner throughout the previous week about his.

I have the impression that a significant proportion of you will be able to recognize yourself in this narrative.

So, what exactly is going on here?

Why does this alteration stemming from wrath and unease occur so frequently?

Relationship in the midst of powerlessness and resentment

Social analyst Leonard Berkowitz (1990) proposes that any unfavorable circumstance that makes an inclination of defenselessness can get to be molded to trigger defensive conditions of anger and animosity. This is due to the fact that people easily learn to partner helplessness with weakness and to relate the adrenaline surge of anger with an inclination of force and control. Any unfavorable circumstance that makes an inclination of defenselessness can get to be molded to trigger defensive conditions of anger and animosity.

Negative sensations such as unease, unhappiness, shame, and self-doubt, to put it in layman's words, may make us feel fragile, incompetent, and vulnerable. A healthy dose of fury may motivate us to take action and strengthen our resolve, even in the face of risk.

Convincing and full of serious thought

In spite of the fact that I knew, on some level, that I had a traumatic experience that made me anxious about going in the snow, and in spite of the fact that I was very much aware as a specialist that anger and uneasiness can be exchanged, what my own experience demonstrated to me is how absolutely convincing and all around legitimized my anger was to me. What my own experience demonstrated to me is how absolutely persuading and all around legitimized my anger was to me.

Taking Care Of Our Families And Children While Keeping Our Tempers In Check

People often believe that people who have children will bring up their offspring in the same manner in which they themselves were brought up. This may be a positive thing as well as a harmful thing, particularly if you were encouraged to repress your feelings or were not given an effective approach to deal with anger by your parents or other role models. When it comes to members of the family, particularly youngsters, it may be challenging to attempt to interrupt long-established routines that are sometimes undesirable. It requires a deliberate effort not to do things that we learnt while growing up that might hamper the emotional intelligence and development of our kid. These are things that we learned from our parents and teachers.

Everyone has overheard their parents saying something along the lines of,

"When I was a kid, we had to walk uphill both ways to get to school." No matter the temperature or the weather, we had no choice but to carry out our duties. A probable exaggeration said to their children in order to impart some wisdom. This is a lesson in life that is aimed to educate children that despite the fact that we may find ourselves in challenging circumstances, we should never give up. Most importantly, if we have a duty, we shouldn't just shrug it off because we think it would be difficult or complex to fulfill.

This is a lesson that, interestingly enough, can be applied to parenting in some way. Being a parent is both one of the most gratifying and one of the most stressful experiences a person can have in their life. If you're a good parent, your kids will be good. Additionally, the inverse is also true. This is a significant burden to bear, particularly considering that individuals are experiencing higher levels of stress now compared to earlier times. According to the results of the

National Survey of America's Families, which was conducted in 1997, 1999, and again in 2007, it was found that the level of annoyance felt by parents throughout the country grew by 20-35% between 1997 and 2007. This figure indicates that parents are likely dealing with an increasing level of stress in their daily lives.

Once upon a time, one parent would go to work while the other parent would remain at home to take care of the house and raise the children. It is now a far more usual occurrence for both parents to maintain full-time jobs. This dynamic is one of the factors that contributes to the anxiety and annoyance that a parent could experience. They are expected to perform at the highest possible level while they are at work, and when they get home, they must maintain that level of performance in order to keep up with their children. After putting the children to bed, it is time to tidy up the home, wash the laundry, and prepare the meals for the following day. It should come as no surprise that parents have a difficult time keeping their emotions in control while dealing with their children.

It is very normal for you to feel upset with your kid or the conduct they exhibit. But if you discover that you are consistently angry with them, then there may be something wrong with the relationship. You probably become aware, in times of relative peace, that your child is only acting in a manner typical of children. That you might be able to be a more effective parent if you were able to maintain your composure more of the time. If you don't experience these feelings, but you're still angry with your children for the way your life has turned out, then there may be another issue at play here.

Contaminated Anger

Anger is almost always associated with unfavorable outcomes, which is something that seems to be a general consensus across all individuals. In point of fact, rage is more detrimental than beneficial. If given the opportunity, negative or destructive rage may wreak havoc and inflict a significant amount of harm; this kind of fury is also referred to as destructive anger. Anger, in addition to being destructive, may also lead to a great deal of health difficulties, on all levels, including the physical, the mental, and the psychological. Anger that is negative or harmful may be directed at other people, but it can also be directed on oneself, depending on how an individual responds to anger as an individual. In any case, it is possible that it may result in emotional and psychological damage, making it harmful. Because anger has a physical impact on the body, someone who struggles with controlling their anger may have symptoms such as a faster heart rate, higher blood pressure, and an increase in adrenaline. Anger is considered to be a secondary emotion, and many times it is the result of a human's response to particular events or persons who have prompted other negative emotions such as despair, loneliness, fear, and a variety of other unfriendly sensations.

Especially in our relationships, personal life, and places of employment, the unpleasant and uncontrolled expressions of rage may have fatal effects. Venting, yelling, or having an outburst is seen by many individuals to be the most effective method to let one's anger to evaporate, despite the fact that many others feel that keeping one's anger bottled up or repressing it is the greatest way to let one's anger die down.

To tell you the truth, however, none of them are appropriate methods for venting your frustration. It doesn't matter whether you bottle it up or let it all out; either way, you'll end up with the same undesirable results. When it reaches its most severe form, destructive rage may result in a wide variety of vices, including assault, marital violence, child abuse, and even criminal behavior. Even if we have established that anger is a secondary response to fear, grief, or even loneliness, the reality of the matter is that the majority of people consider being angry to be a very normal occurrence. This is due to the fact that the majority of people grew up in an atmosphere where it is acceptable, and as a result, they lose touch with how to regulate their anger.

Even though we claim that it is OK to express anger and that anger may be beneficial, this is not the case for negative anger. The reason for this is that persons who struggle to manage their anger and who get upset even when there is no apparent reason to do so are more likely to be classified as having negative or destructive anger. After then, the person's anger has a tendency to make them behave in an unreasonable and illogical manner, despite the fact that they do not want to. After they have worked through their anger, the vast majority of the time is when they realize they have done something regrettable or incorrect. It's true that rage is destructive and bad, but there are many different reasons why people perceive this to be the case. The following are some of these reasons:

Problems In Controlling One's Anger May Manifest Itself In A Variety Of Psychological Ways.

Some people have explosive outbursts, while others may pout and retreat from social situations. Finally, there are some people who have a tendency to repress their anger or engage in self-injurious behavior in attempt to calm it down. As a culture, we do not look askance at expressing feelings such as love, empathy, pleasure, sorrow, or even mourning since there is no stigma attached to doing so. On the other hand, people often group anger along with other bad emotions such as envy, jealousy, and spite. Emotions that are not socially acceptable or accepted are ones that we learn to suppress while we are young. As a consequence of this, we choose to bury our feelings of resentment with the feelings of shame, guilt, and devastation that our wrath had engendered. A person who struggles with anger management may have low self-esteem as a result of feeling sorrow for their outbursts of rage. People don't truly understand why they behaved the way they did most of the time, so how can they expect others to comprehend why they did what they did? Anger may leave a person feeling raw, just as any other emotional condition does, and the knowledge that they have inflicted their misery on others can make the sensation much worse. The majority of people who struggle with difficulties related to anger management will not seek treatment or even know where to begin attempting to improve their situation because they fear being judged or the sensation of being socially isolated. While others, rather than admitting that they too could be the source of the issue, place the blame on the subject or target of their ire.

For those who are going through emotional struggles of any type, it may be difficult to acknowledge those struggles or to speak about them. Fear is one of the most prevalent underlying causes of emotional problems, and it not only contributes to the severity of these problems but also discourages individuals from seeking professional assistance. It is also a fantastic motivator for the individual to get therapy, particularly if they are afraid of losing everything and everyone they love. When you find it difficult to control your anger, this may start to have an influence on your mental and emotional wellness, which may express in a variety of different ways. It's possible that you believe you have everything under control, but there are several warning signals that might indicate otherwise.

Reformat Your Thought Process

When someone is furious, they often say things that are both unreasonable and bad, and it is not uncommon to hear them doing so.

They insult the intelligence of others and speak negatively to themselves in a variety of ways, telling oneself things like "I can't do this anymore!" I can't take it anymore!" People have the misconception that doing this would help them calm down, but the reality is that it just makes their anger worse.

There will be moments when you feel as if none of your efforts are being recognized or acknowledged, when it seems as though the whole world is conspiring against you, and when you just want to give up.

When this occurs, the second stage in anger management is to reframe your thinking about the situation. Cognitive restructuring, also known as re-channeling your thinking, is an approach that is effective in the same way that optimism is. It is necessary for you to reorganize your negative ideas into ones that are more sensible and positive.

It is not necessary for cognitive restructuring to take place only during the rage episode. You may also use this strategy if you are experiencing negative emotions such as tension, depression, or anxiety.

You may also use cognitive restructuring to plan how you will regulate your anger in the future. To do this, just create scenarios in your mind that will cause you to feel angry or anxious, and then think about how you will deal with those situations.

Using the scenario from the previous chapter as a guide, how can you use cognitive restructuring to keep your cool when you're angry? After determining the extent of your rage, you should make an effort to reason with yourself in order to calm down.

Instead of focusing on exacting vengeance on the person who hit you, attempt to come up with reasons why you shouldn't continue doing what it is that you are about to do. This will help you avoid more negative consequences.

To begin, there is no use in giving him a blow in return. It will not help the situation and will only make it worse. It is quite likely that he will hit you once more. Second, giving him a blow in return will injure your hands.

You probably don't want a bruise on your knuckles later on, do you? And third, giving him a punch in return would simply make you more enraged. It is a potential additional cause of stress.

Cognitive restructuring not only helps you avoid getting into problems, but it also makes it easier for you to lead a life free of stress. For instance, you are frustrated because you did not do well enough on your test to pass it.

People's typical method of venting their rage by tearing their tests to pieces and resolving not to study for the topic in question again in the future is to do both of these things. However, engaging in these activities will only get you more into difficulty.

If you choose to participate in these activities, you can expect to get lesser marks. Before you can effectively cope with your anger, you must first identify the factors that contributed to your missteps.

Don't blame the other people in your life or yourself for what occurred. Instead, you should inquire as to what may have gone wrong during the procedure and what steps you might take to prevent it from happening again in the future.

Try not to focus on your past errors and instead learn from what you did wrong. You should acknowledge that you are feeling unhappy, but you also need to be aware that there is another thing that you can do to stop it from occurring again in the future.

Learn To Master Your Angry Feelings Before They Master You.

When you're angry, it's easy to believe that your feelings are beyond of your control because of how intense and chaotic they become.

Learn how to keep it under control.

A sense of rage

Keeping control of your anger

Anger is something that everyone has felt at some time in their lives, whether it was a momentary irritation or a full-blown wrath.

The human feeling of anger is one that is completely normal and, in most cases, beneficial.

On the other hand, when it gets out of hand and starts to do damage, it may lead to problems that lower the quality of your life in general, as well as the quality of your relationships with other people and your professional life.

When you're angry, it's easy to believe that your feelings are beyond of your control because of how intense and chaotic they become.

How can we define anger?

The qualities that anger has

An expert in the field of psychology who specializes in the study of anger describes anger as "an emotional state that ranges in intensity from mild irritation to intense fury and rage."

Changes in one's body, both physiological and biochemical, accompany the experience of rage, just as they do with other emotions. For example, when you become angry, your blood pressure, heart rate, and levels of the chemicals that give you energy, noradrenaline, and adrenaline, all rise. This is because anger causes your sympathetic nervous system to produce more of these hormones.

Anger may be provoked by both the outside world and by one's own thoughts and actions.

It's possible that you're irritated with a specific person (like a colleague or boss) or scenario (like a traffic congestion or a canceled trip) rather than with your own worries or ruminations about your own problems. This might be the source of your anger.

Remembering frightening or distressing events may sometimes bring up feelings of rage in certain people.

Manifestation of rage

The instinctive and natural method to deal with rage is to lash out with physical force.

Anger is a natural and adaptive response to dangers; it causes powerful and often violent sentiments and actions, which equip us to fight and protect ourselves in the event that we are attacked.

Therefore, rage is, to some degree, necessary for our continued existence.

However, because to laws, societal standards, and just plain common sense, there are limits to how far our rage may go. We are not able to engage in a violent confrontation with each and every person or object that causes us irritation or annoyance.

People use a number of conscious and unconscious coping mechanisms to get over their furious sentiments and go on with their lives.

The three primary coping mechanisms are known as "expressing," "repressing," and "calming."

When venting your frustration, it's best to do it in a manner that is firm but not confrontational. This will help you feel better faster.

In order to accomplish this goal, you will need to hone your ability to articulate your requirements concisely and locate accommodating solutions to satisfy them.

Being assertive does not imply acting aggressively or being demanding; rather, it entails respecting both yourself and the people around you.

The pent-up rage that has been repressed has the potential to be redirected or transformed.

This is what occurs when you are able to control your anger, push it out of your mind, and instead focus your attention on something productive.

The goal is to gain control of, or at least suppress, your anger and redirect it into acts that are more productive.

The danger that comes with this sort of response is that if it isn't given the opportunity to be expressed outwardly, it may shift inside and be directed against the person who is causing it, which is you.

Anger that is kept to oneself might lead to mental health issues such as depression or high blood pressure.

Anger that is not properly channeled might lead to other problems.

It may lead to pathological outbursts of anger, such as engaging in passive-aggressive conduct (getting back at someone discreetly without explaining why rather than addressing them directly) or developing a personality that is unflinchingly hostile.

People who constantly tear people down, criticize everything, and make cynical comments have not yet learned how to cope with their anger in a healthy manner.

It is not unexpected that they won't have too many relationships that end up being joyful for them.

You are at last able to rest on the inside.

This means exercising control not just over your outward conduct but also over your internal responses, taking measures to slow down your heartbeat, calming yourself down, and allowing the emotions to run through you naturally.

If none of these three strategies are effective, "Someone—or something—is going to get hurt," according to the proverb.

Keeping control of your rage

Anger management has two primary goals: one is to reduce the emotional sensations that anger creates, and the other is to reduce the physiological arousal that anger causes.

Because the things or people that annoy you cannot be changed, it is impossible to get rid of them or avoid encountering them. On the other hand, you may train yourself to regulate your responses.

Respect For The Fury Expressed By Others

It is just as vital for you to learn how to respect other people's anger, especially the fury of those who are close to you. While our primary emphasis has been on teaching you how to honor your anger and modify your unhealthy anger style, it is equally as critical that you learn how to honor other people's anger. To be successful in this endeavor, I advise that you study the sections of this book that discuss the various expressions of rage and figure out which style best describes each member of your family. The ideas and information presented in this chapter will be of assistance as well. The first section of this chapter will concentrate on providing you with broad knowledge that you may use to understand how to cope with the anger of other people, regardless of the manner in which those other individuals express their anger. In the next section of the chapter, I will provide you with tailored guidance for dealing with a number of the various rage types. It is just as vital for you to learn how to respect other people's anger, especially the fury of those who are close to you. While our primary emphasis has been on teaching you how to honor your anger and modify your unhealthy anger style, it is equally as critical that you learn how to honor other people's anger. To be successful in this endeavor, I advise that you study the sections of this book that discuss the various expressions of rage and figure out which style best describes each member of your family.

The ideas and information presented in this chapter will be of assistance as well. The first section of this chapter will concentrate on providing you with broad knowledge that you may use to understand how to cope with the anger of other people, regardless of the manner in which those other individuals express their anger. In the next section of the chapter, I will provide you with tailored guidance for dealing with a number of the various rage types. We are usually able to let go of our anger once we have the sense that the other person has heard us, comprehended what we have to say, and feels for us. On the other hand, if we get the impression that the other person is not listening to what we have to say, we are more inclined to hold onto our anger or even to feel it intensify.

If you really want to find a solution to a disagreement with another person, the most crucial thing you can do is pay close attention while that person explains the source of her anger to you. Do not engage in a debate with her, do not interrupt her, do not act defensive, and do not make fun of her for being furious. Listen to what she has to say. You may improve your listening abilities by adopting the following mentalities and developing the following talents:

Attend Closely and Listen

An active listener is someone who shows interest in what the other person is saying as well as care for how they are feeling about what they are saying. If you merely provide the appearance of listening, you won't deceive anybody, and you will foster sentiments of resentment and distrust instead. Stop whatever else you're doing and direct all of your attention and energy into the person you're talking to so that you can really hear what they have to say. Maintain eye contact as much as you can and give the speaker the occasional nod to indicate that you are listening to and comprehending what is being stated.

Assume the other person is acting in a morally upright manner.

Instead of considering the other person to be an adversary, a good listener operates on the assumption that they are acting in a non-hostile manner. He thinks the other person must have a valid cause for being angry, and despite the fact that he does not approve of the way the other person is behaving, he does not think the other person is a horrible person.

Keep an open mind while you listen.

Listen without attaching any value judgments to what is being said in order to have a complete understanding of the other person and the circumstances behind the disagreement. Listen with a sense of wonder in your heart. Make an effort to get across the word, "I respect you. I care about what you think and how you feel, regardless of whether or not I agree with what you say.

Taking Pleasure In Seeing Children Thrive

Children are enchanting creatures in their own right. They are created in a wonderful manner by erupting from a little assemblage of cells. We don't always appreciate the advantage we have of being able to see one of life's genuine miracles unfold.

On the surface, it is not always simple to see how children grow and progress throughout time. Under the hood, there are dozens of different processes working in tandem to keep everything running smoothly. Children are given the opportunity to develop the abilities necessary to lead meaningful lives thanks to these procedures.

You may be startled to learn that children's development does not follow linear or predictable patterns, especially if you were under the impression that it does. Children almost never develop in a linear fashion. Along the journey, there are a number of unexpected turns and twists. Nevertheless, broad markers assist us in determining the overall developmental phases that a kid goes through throughout their lifetime.

That is the topic that we are going to talk about today.

This chapter will address the ways in which children's developmental routes are similar to one another while yet being distinct. While examining the primary phases of development that children go through, we will also place an emphasis on the individuality of each kid.

Before we go any further, there is something very important that I want you to bear in mind. Every single youngster has an astounding variety of abilities and strengths. They have the ability to develop into practically whatever they set their minds to being, and their potential is virtually limitless. Therefore, it is up to us to assist them in realizing their potential so that they may develop into the magnificent beings that they are intended to be.

When we have a solid grasp of our children's developmental stages, we are better able to comprehend their behaviors and emotions. It enables us to realize that our children behave the way that they do to convey their requirements according to the stage of development that they are now in. Having an understanding of the many phases of development that our children go through is similar to having a road map to our children's minds. Having this understanding will make a significant dent in the frustration and rage that you feel. It is my hope that by the time you reach the conclusion of this chapter, you will have realized that many of the most difficult experiences that your children go through are just a natural part of their growth.

Are you prepared to go?

Let's just get right in, shall we?

TAKING INTO ACCOUNT YOUR TRIGGERS

A person's conduct may be influenced by a number of different circumstances, which are referred to as triggers. They play the role of catalysts.

The failure to get what was requested or an insensitive remark from a complete stranger are two examples of potential triggers.

An incident that sets off a teenager's anxiety can be the spreading of rumors about them by a friend or acquaintance.

It is essential to have an understanding of what causes you to become angry in order to develop effective anger management skills. What gets your blood to boiling point, infuriates you, and aggravates you the most? All of these are potential triggers.

It is not sufficient to only keep track of these things in your head; you must also write it down.

You should also be aware that interactions with other people do not always result in rage. Anger, and most of the time hostility, might be triggered by the situation in which we find ourselves at times. Anger may be triggered by a variety of factors, including noise and air pollution, such as what a person who lives in an industrial or construction zone might experience. Sometimes, this happens without our knowing.

You feel like snapping right now because of the way the atmosphere is.

Anger is another emotion that may result from stress. The global globe moves at a breakneck pace, and as a result, we are impacted by it. The persistent irritation and anger that you experience might be a result of stress.

If you are unsure as to why you are furious, you should pay attention to your surroundings and determine whether or not you obtain a enough amount of tranquility.

Individual behaviors, such as engaging in aggressive entertainment, such as viewing or reading about violent movies or literature, not getting enough sleep, or becoming intoxicated, may also serve as catalysts for the onset of aggressive behavior.

It is also essential to keep in mind that people are more likely to get angry when they are feeling hungry. Anger may be avoided to some extent by eating the appropriate number of meals on a regular basis.

There are a lot of things that might set us off and all of them are considered to be triggers. Finding out what your trigger is can help you cope with it in a more targeted manner. There is a proverb that goes, "Knowing the problem is half the solution." This is a very true statement.

Anger And Its Effects On Your Mental Health

One more thing we should discuss here is the idea of anger and how it can affect your mental health. In some cases, violence will not be a disorder on its own. For some people, chronic irritation is something they need to work on and can learn to manage, but for others, anger could mean that there is another mental disorder that needs treatment.

When a therapist is trying to assess the danger that is happening. There are a few different mental conditions strictly related to violence, and they all need to be explored to see if they may also be part of the problem. Some of the most common mental conditions that are related to anger include:

1. Bipolar disorder: One of the common characteristics of mania in this type of

disease will be irritability. A person may have symptoms of anger when they enter one of the depressive phases.

2. Major depression: Anger may be directed at others or yourself during this time.

3. Narcissistic personality disorder. Someone who considers himself a narcissist can lash out at anger if he feels that someone else is attacking his ego. They will use this anger to generate some of the other feelings they have, including inferiority and fear.

4. Oppositional defiant behavior: Angry and hostile behavior is one of the main signs of ODD in children.

5. Post Traumatic Stress Disorder: Post Traumatic Stress Disorder will often lead to an outbreak of anger, and this can often happen without any provocation. Stress will push the person to the limit so that the mind can no longer function usually.

Many different things will happen to the body when you experience a lot of anger regularly. Having a little passion sometimes is not a bad thing, and can help improve your life. However, if you allow that anger to linger without giving you the care and attention you need, then you will run into some severe problems, like many of which we discuss in this guide.

The Ten-Step Process That Will Take You From Discord To Harmony

Something to keep in mind is something that is pretty easy, but yet we constantly seem to forget it...the likely cause of conflict in any relationship is misunderstanding that occurred between the parties. Expectations that don't meet reality, or simply plain insensitivity. What makes the difference is when you are aware and then actively make the effort to stop the 'blood flow before it renders you unconscious'...yes, this is a rather graphic analogy, but I think you get the point. It is always preferable to take preventative measures rather than attempt to discover a cure.

The restoration of peace in the midst of potentially explosive circumstances does not need brain surgery; rather, all that is required are a few basic measures that, when taken together, may make all the difference in the world. These steps are not always straightforward to do, but the benefits of doing so will more than justify the effort. It will demonstrate how sensitive you are, how open you are, and how conscious you are of what the other person is feeling, thinking, or saying.

I want you to do something right now, and that something is to get rid of the assumption that conflict in any relationship is necessarily "bad" and an indication that something is "wrong" with the relationship. I want you to get rid of that belief right now. It is impossible to avoid conflict.

When two individuals decide to form a love connection with one another, they each carry with them a lifetime's worth of individual experiences, hopes, expectations, and beliefs. People sometimes refer to this as "baggage"...yes, that's a bit of an exaggeration but fine, it provides a picture of what each person brings with them to every relationship.

Your perspective is not always superior or inferior to that of your spouse; rather, it is only distinct from theirs. Think about it: if you were brought up in the same setting as that person, with the same parents, with the same biological predispositions, you would be a totally different person than the one you are right now.

It's just a matter of trying to tackle problems from a new angle. Even if you put forth your very best effort, you cannot prevent conflicts from occurring. It is a process of development since the occurrence of these events propels the connection to the subsequent degree of development.

The main drawback of having disagreements is that they almost always result in bruised emotions and regrets. Instead, we need to look at these disagreements as a kind of feedback and an aspect of our situation that calls for us to make improvements or adjustments.

It takes a deliberate decision on your behalf to show empathy, whether it's toward your relationship or toward other people. Reflect on your own life experiences as well as the probable triggers that the other person is carrying with them, as well as the life experiences that they have had. It is important to keep in mind that even though you accept and understand the conduct of your spouse, this does not always indicate that you condone or would tolerate such behavior. This is where the vital 'edge' of loving communication is required to break down barriers to peace and pave the way for the development of meaningful connections between people.

Everyone can turn a difficult situation into a chance to get closer to one another and improve their relationship, rather than allowing the disagreement to tear it apart. One of the things that awareness accomplishes is that it helps widen your viewpoint and enables you to make advantage of these possibilities to manage conflict in a more effective manner than you did in the past. It does this by providing internal clues such as tension, anger, worry, or discomfort; it also gives exterior cues such as your partner retreating, defending, or attacking.

If you are able to anticipate when a fight could break out between the two of you, you will have the opportunity to sort things out together, which will strengthen your connection, help you sympathize with one another, and open up more channels of communication between the two of you.

Take a look at it with me.

Tips That Will Help Your Young Child Feel Less Angry

As a parent, you have many responsibilities, but one of the most important ones is to assist your toddler with comprehending and communicating their emotions in appropriate and non-aggressive ways. This is not a straightforward endeavor. It takes a very long time and a great deal of patience to accomplish. Nevertheless, over the next several months and years, with your encouragement and help, your kid will learn to regulate their strong emotions and the responses they have to them. The following three-step strategy is usually met with positive responses from youngsters.

The first step is to watch and take notes.

Your consideration of the following questions will assist you in identifying patterns and determining the fundamental reasons behind your child's behaviour. You are going to put this information to use in order to choose the most effective strategy to implement.

What exactly is going on in your kid's life right now? Where exactly is the conduct being exhibited? Home? Where can I find day care? Where is the mall? Where is Grandma's house? Is it occurring everywhere or the majority of the time that your youngster goes? If it just happens in one place, the environment (such as being too busy, too bright, or too overpowering, for example) is usually what's triggering the behavior. Is the course of action directed at a specific person or a limited number of participants? Is the child's temper tantrum sometimes directed towards someone who is in close proximity to the child? When is the most probable time for the event to take place? For example, just before your child's nap time, when they are already worn out? During times of change, such as when you're moving from one activity to another? It is usual practice to cite these types of pressures as potential reasons of aggressive conduct.

What transpired in the moments leading up to the difficult conduct shown by your child? For instance, had you just informed everyone that it was time to stop playing the game and get in the car? They looked around in confusion, wondering whether another youngster had just taken one of their toys. Is there a recent development in their life that has made them feel agitated, out of control, or unhappy, or that has made them feel less safe and secure in general? Your kid may feel uncomfortable as a consequence of a new room at child care, a move to a new house, the arrival of a new baby, or the loss of a family pet. As a result, your child may be less able to control their impulses.

SUMMARY OF THE INTERACTIVE COMPONENT

Both the factors that might lead to anger and the strategies for coping with it have been discussed.

If you suspect that your anger may be a sign of an underlying mental condition or if you learnt to be angry as a kid, however, it may be beneficial for you to see a therapist in order to develop a more permanent strategy for controlling your anger.

Second, as was said earlier, you need to make it a priority to lower the amount of stress in your life. You should work on being able to say "no" as "often as" you say "yes." Accept the fact that you will never be able to do everything at once, no matter how much you value productivity. It would be to your advantage to let go of certain things. Cut down on your obligations as much as you can. A more tranquil house is directly proportional to mental clarity.

The third step is to start keeping a gratitude notebook. Every night before you go to sleep, jot down three things—especially about your child—that have made you happy that day. It may be something as little as how many hours of sleep you received that day or as significant as how happy your kid was throughout the day.

In conclusion, you need to plan up a program for your nutrition and your workout routine. You will find that you have less anger over time as a result of the fact that both of these hobbies assist lessen the amount of stress in your life.

Passion may be the most appropriate word to use to describe an angry reaction that is both spontaneous and productive. In most cases, raw emotion and/or physical discomfort are the driving forces for passionate expressiveness. This is a spontaneous and instantaneous reaction to the fury that I feel. When the trigger for your anger is something that hits on something you have strong emotions about, your ideals, or your values, you are more likely to experience passion as a consequence.

There is still some evidence of self-control, and it is probable that sentiments and expectations will be communicated. On the other hand, those who vent their rage in this manner can come to the conclusion that they are unable to deal with it in a constructive manner. In this case, they might seek a time-out in order to gather their thoughts before proceeding to find a solution to the problem at hand. There is yet hope for a successful conclusion.

You'll know you're seeing rage when the person's reaction to their fury is both impulsive and damaging. The overly dramatic and intensely emotional reaction known as rage. It's possible that a traumatic event from your past is the source of this. It was not anticipated, and in most cases, it is not beneficial.

Rage is perhaps the most archetypical and representative form of expressing rage. You are quite likely to hear shouting and swearing, and there is a possibility that you may see conduct that is threatening, aggressive, abusive, and even violent. In the workplace, rage of this kind is both counterproductive and detrimental, and it should never be condoned.

What Is It?

Try to match the many ways of expressing anger with the attributes linked with them. There is a possibility that more than one characteristic will be matched to each expression type.

Alternate Meanings:

A. Unplanned and Creatively Constructed B. Targets that Erupt on Their Own and Are Destructive:

1. Instigated by ardor and strong emotions

2. An emotional reaction that is impulsive, excessive, and often

explosive. 3. may need a little rest and relaxation break at times

4. It is sometimes used as an alibi for venting one's wrath.

A response

Because it is ignited by fervor and intense emotions, an instantaneous outburst of rage that is both beneficial and unplanned occurs almost instantly.

A person is said to be raging when they vent their anger in a way that is both impulsive and damaging. Aggression is often irrational and overstated.

When one's expression of rage is spontaneous and productive, while at the same time being generally courteous and sensible, one's capacity for self-control is reduced. It may result in a time-out, in which case a settlement would be sought at a later date.

Rage is the outcome of spontaneously expressing anger in a harmful manner, and it is possible that anything might be used as a reason for erupting into wrath at any given moment.

In this moment, Abigail is delivering a presentation to a prospective customer. Things aren't going as smoothly as she would want them to be going right now. Because her business partner, Mike, was meant to be here to assist with the complicated presentation, Abigail is preoccupied as a result. Not only does she have to do everything on her own, but she is also upset with Mike, which is preventing her from concentrating on her presentation.

Examine each of the potential outbursts of fury that Abigail may make when she discovers Mike.

You Have A Choice In How You Express Your Anger.

Because displaying anger is always a choice, it does not always need to be a negative one. When we are angry, the majority of us, unfortunately, follow the route that has been taken the most, which is to lash out. While this may seem like the simpler approach at first, it really has lasting ramifications that make life a lot more challenging.

The display of wrath may be something that you learnt as a kid from a caregiver, or it may be something that is driven by inherited genetics. However, expressions of rage that originated from your environment or from DNA may be controlled if they are given sufficient attention. Becoming a steady force in an unpredictable environment is a major accomplishment, and you should look forward to the progression toward greater control, more enjoyment, and more productivity as a result of this success.

Poor for one's health Displays of Angry Emotions

A painful scenario gives rise to an angry emotion, which then develops into an outburst or the repression of sentiments in an attempt to modify the situation. Unproductive displays of anger begin with a painful event that gives rise to the furious emotion. These strategies result in a greater amount of friction because they are met with resistance from the opposing side, and that resistance results in a greater amount of discomfort.

Frequently, when people are angry, they will resort to one of the following harmful options:

Suppression occurs when an individual does not express any reaction to their feelings of rage. This is not an act of passive hostility; rather, it is an effort by someone to look flawless and not reveal weakness, an attempt not to be impolite, or the individual does not want to put another problem on top of the existing challenging circumstance. They may even argue against the idea that they are furious, but on the inside, they are seething, and those fumes are poisonous. It is an indication of rigidity, self-consciousness, or the desire for acceptance and approval when someone suppresses their feelings.

It's true that passive aggression is a sort of suppression, but the person who engages in it isn't trying to appear stoic or deny that they're angry. Passive aggressive behavior is a form of suppression. Instead, they are venting their ire in a way that is counterproductive, but they are making the conscious decision not to lose control of their emotions and erupt, reveal their vulnerabilities, or say something they may come to regret in the heat of the moment. Their covert rage manifests itself as a refusal to communicate or cooperate, as well as as sulking, sabotaging, evading, and taking out their frustration on others. This is a game of control and superiority, but it doesn't solve anything, and it only makes the other person more angry.

Aggression directed outward: Many people conflate anger with wrath, and the reason for this association is open hostility, which may occasionally escalate into physical violence, as well as emotional or mental abuse. While repressing anger and engaging in passive aggressive behavior are both bad responses to frustration, engaging in immature, outward forms of violence may destroy lives and take on a criminal dimension in many instances. The openly aggressive person adopts a firm position to gain ground at the price of another person, displaying either no or very little empathy and a total lack of sensitivity. This is done at the expense of the other person.

Their requirements and beliefs are more significant than those of other individuals, and they take precedence over them. They will resort to violent means in order to prove their arguments, such as intimidation, pointing the finger of blame, mocking, teasing, explosive conduct, and deceit or illegal activities. The use of sarcasm, condescension, harsh criticism, and persistent whining are all examples of open forms of aggressiveness that are more subtle.

Aggression against others is often the result of insecurity, a lack of empathy, and an unrealistic pursuit of perfectionism. This kind of person is needy, and they demand that they and their ideas deserve respect. There will be no peace until everyone is in perfect line with this type of person's concept of perfection, despite the fact that this type of person is imperfect.

Handling Children's Angry Emotions

The primary objective of anger management is to lessen the severity of one's responses when furious. You need to have a lot of patience with your kid just as you would with them learning everything else there is to learn. You also need to be conscious that every person is an individual with their own set of circumstances and a distinct pace at which they acquire new things.

You should make it your mission to assist your kid in expressing anger in a manner that is forceful rather than confrontational. This indicates that kids should not learn how to stifle their anger but rather how to manage with it when it arises.

Once you have an understanding of what anger is, how to recognize it, and the factors that contribute to anger in both you and your kid, it is often much easier to exercise proper anger management. Recognizing what causes your anger is the first step in anger management.

Explore the possibility of uncovering the source of your child's ire. You have the option of going to a psychologist to find out whether there are any underlying biological or developmental factors that are contributing to your anger. Eliminate the possibility of any kind of learning difficulty or even allergies. These factors might be contributing to the outbursts of rage that your kid has recently shown.

After eliminating the possibility of biological causes, the next step is to investigate the possibility of environmental influences. You should be able to recall the environmental conditions that we were subjected to. It's possible that these problems stem from too high standards imposed either at school or at home.

It's also possible that the parents are going through a difficult time due to a recent traumatic experience, such as an accident or even a divorce. When you are attempting to determine the causes of your child's anger, one of the most crucial factors to take into consideration is the life pressures that they are experiencing.

Is it first thing in the morning when he or she wakes up, or does it happen while they are playing? Consider the setting in which he vents his rage; is it at home or at school? Is there a certain individual that brings on the outburst of rage? What are some of the experiences that the family has had in the recent past or is going through at this time? Is it possible that one of these occurrences is having an effect on the child?

After you've identified the precipitating factor, you should work to address the underlying problem. Remove the underlying cause if at all feasible. However, while you are doing this, keep in mind that your kid has already formed the habit. Because of this, an important element of your strategy should be to teach your child how to control their anger and assist them through the process.

During this stage of the procedure, the following are the essential points to keep in mind:

Do not make an effort to prevent your kid from being angry; as we have seen, becoming angry is a natural process that all human beings are required to go through at some point in their lives. Our objective is to teach your kid how to cope with this feeling rather than to teach them to repress it in any way.

When a youngster is taught to stifle their anger, it might have negative consequences for them as they become older.

Assist your kid in locating alternate methods of coping with anger; while instructing our children in alternative methods of coping with anger, we need to take their ages into consideration. If they are teens, it will be much simpler to have a conversation with them about other methods in which they might reduce their core body temperature.

This may be accomplished by isolating oneself for a period of time until they have regained their composure. Some people find that pounding a pillow helps them feel better. There is a wide range of topics that may be discussed with either him or her. I will walk you through the processes of helping the younger ones achieve self-control as I accompany you as you work with them.

The Warning Signs Of Rage That Cannot Be Suppressed

The never-ending frustration that results from not being able to control your actions and seeing your life fall apart is, without a doubt, overwhelming. The following is a list of red flags that you should be on the lookout for if you are unsure as to whether or not the instability in your life is the result of difficulties with your conduct. If you find that you suffer many of them, you need to persuade yourself to take the courageous step of engaging in anger management and, if necessary, seeking professional therapy.

Are you experiencing more anger than the situation warrants? You realize that you are yelling excessively over the most insignificant of issues, worrying about it beyond the matter at hand, and feeling upset about everything and everything connected to it.

Finding it difficult to let go of the sensation — Even after the little issue that you were upset about has been resolved, you continue to feel dissatisfied and agitated for a considerable amount of time, and you are unable to act normally with anybody until the feeling passes.

Participating in acts of physical violence - Participating in any type of physical aggression is a severe form of the latter, and steps need to be done to cease it as soon as possible.

Failure to identify the specific causes – It's not always clear to you why you're feeling so upset. their are moments when you just feel impatient and frustrated without their being any clear cause.

You are aware that you have a problem and that you often regret it; nonetheless, you continue to be unsuccessful in finding a solution to the issue, which leads to you feeling even more disappointed with yourself.

It's difficult for you to communicate how you're feeling to other people because you get the impression that they don't get it. Your loved ones often get the mistaken impression that you do not care about them, which is not the case; you just can't seem to stop the destructive conduct you exhibit toward them.

misuse of substances - You have turned to, or at least thought about succumbing to, smoking, drinking, or other forms of substance misuse in order to get rid of the persistent, nagging frustration that is in the back of your mind.

Interference with everyday life - It is essential that you investigate anything that creates obstacles in your way of life on a daily basis. In the event that your performance at work is deteriorating, your significant other is experiencing dissatisfaction, and/or you seem to be losing friends as a result of your conduct, the latter has to be controlled as soon as possible.

Your Health And Your Anger

As was said before, when you become angry, your brain reacts by generating an excessive amount of the hormones cortisol and adrenaline. These hormones are released in response to a variety of emotions, including fear, anxiety, and excitement. The extra cortisol and adrenaline that are produced from the adrenal glands flood the body, and your brain instantly sends more blood to your muscles because it considers that you are in a "fight or flight" scenario. When the adrenal glands are stimulated, the body prepares to either fight or flee.

If this premise is correct, then it follows that the body will get itself ready for some kind of imminent physical activity. As your core temperature begins to increase, you may also notice that you start to perspire. Your blood pressure will rise, your heart rate will accelerate, and you will experience a shift in your breathing pattern.

If the alterations are just temporary, then there is no need for concern. Those who have difficulty managing their anger, on the other hand, seldom experience fleeting bouts of rage.

If you consistently expose your body to high levels of stress hormones like cortisol and adrenaline, this may wreak havoc on your physical health. It will result in significant alterations to the metabolic process and may cause the following problems:

An increase in the frequency and severity of headaches An increase in the frequency and severity of migraines Depression Anxiety Insomnia Irritable bowel syndrome Changes in appetite Weight Changes Acne or eczema Heart

attack or other heart-related conditions
Stroke

Research has even shown that excessive amounts of stress hormones might add to an individual's likelihood of developing cancer.

There are normally two responses to anger for the individual who is feeling it: outburst and suppression. Both of these responses are normal. It is common for people to engage in aggressive or physically destructive actions after allowing themselves to experience "fits of rage." In addition to this, it has a detrimental impact on one's self-esteem and the interpersonal connections of those around them. Meanwhile, concealing your anger almost always results in feelings of melancholy and anxiety, difficulty communicating with other people, and the breakdown of relationships with other people.

Laughter is a great alternative to anger, so try it out!

There are a lot of different ways in which other people might provoke your anger. But instead of responding to them with anger, why not attempt to see whether there is anything hilarious or entertaining about what they are doing? You may be surprised to find that there is. If you can use a few of the suggestions that we discussed earlier in this handbook, then you will be able to calm down and have a greater chance of succeeding in making this happen. However, this will seem to be difficult to do while you are in the thick of the situation; however, if you can utilize these tips when you are in the heat of the moment, then it will look impossible to complete. If you are able to make light of the circumstance, it means that you are prepared to move on and will not allow it have as much of an impact on you.

You will be able to maintain all of that optimism if you are able to see the event in a humorous way, and this will also enable you to feel less frustrated by the many challenges you face in life. This holds true not just for the here and now but also for the future in the event that an identical circumstance arises again.

When it comes to every circumstance that you find yourself in, there is always something to laugh about; all you need to do is learn how to make this happen. You have the ability to chuckle at how wonderful the day is, how ridiculous it is for you to be feeling so upset about what is going on, and a great deal more.

However, in order to successfully complete this procedure, you need set aside some time. If you are someone who has a very poor temper and really needs to work on it a little bit more, then you should not begin with this approach right from the beginning since it is not the technique that you should start with. However, you may work your way up to this one, and you will quickly discover how powerful it can be.

The act of laughing does have a psychological impact on our physical selves. Laughter has been shown to be effective in reducing stress, and as a result, it helps us feel more at ease and comfortable. On the other side, experiencing anger all the time is often associated with long-term mental health conditions such as anxiety, depression, eating disorder, sleeping problem, loneliness, and phobias. Your feelings of anger are simply going to make you feel worse, guilty, and miserable. Therefore, you should constantly make an effort to find the humor even in the most trying of circumstances. Master the art of laughter, don't sweat the little stuff, and train yourself to see the silver lining in every cloud.

www.ingramcontent.com/pod-product-compliance
Lightning Source LLC
Chambersburg PA
CBHW050419120526
44590CB00015B/2034